Can You Help Me?

Jullie Searor

To order additional copies of this book, contact:
Xlibris
844-714-8691
www.Xlibris.com
Orders@Xlibris.com

ISBN: Softcover   978-1-4535-0856-5
        EBook   978-1-6641-5658-6

Library of Congress Control Number: 2010907427

Print information available on the last page

Rev. date: 02/04/2021

Grandma says you need to
cross your heart and pull
it tight.

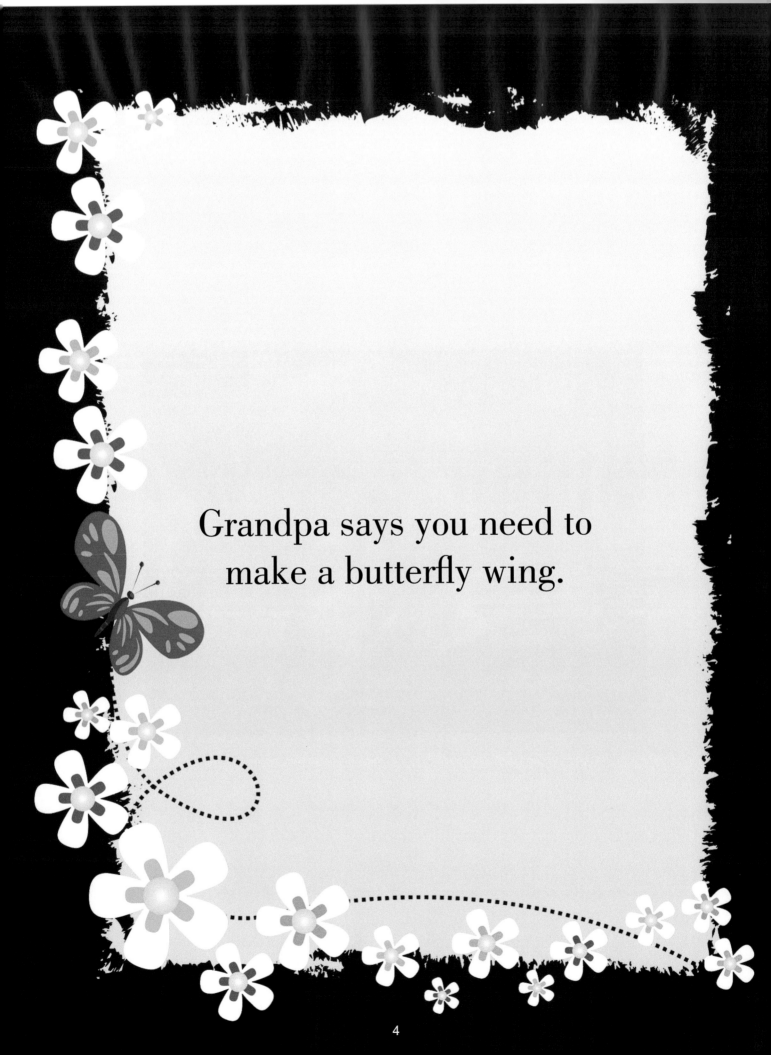

Grandpa says you need to make a butterfly wing.

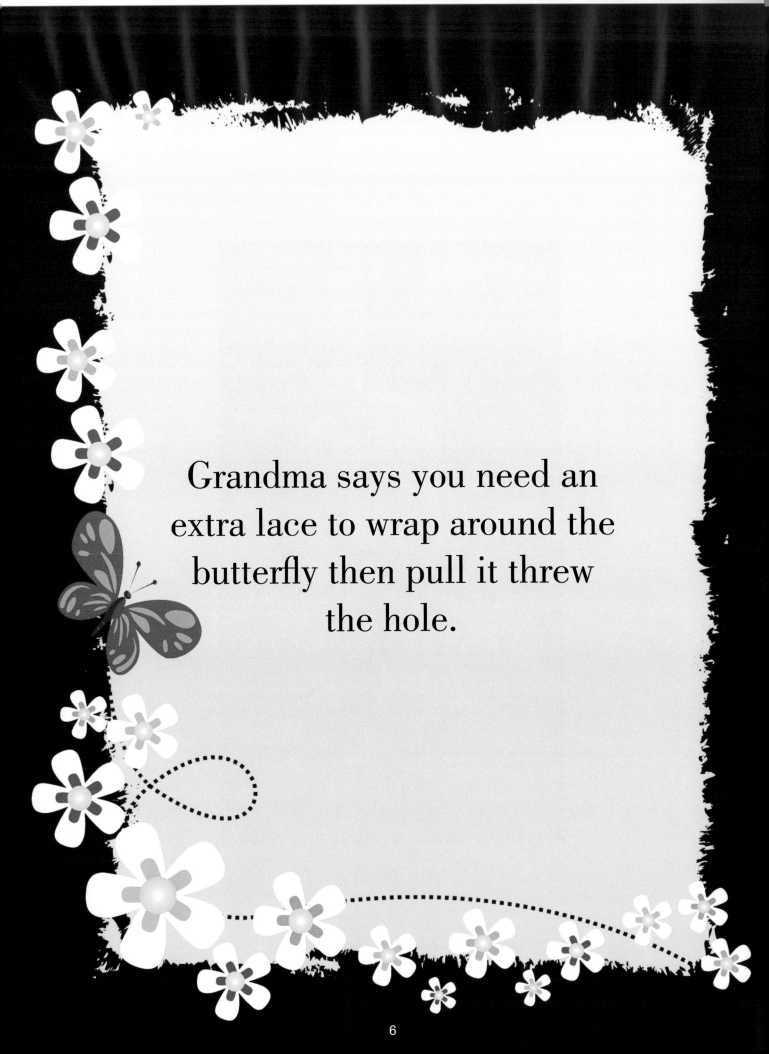

Grandma says you need an extra lace to wrap around the butterfly then pull it threw the hole.

Grandma says if you pull the butterfly wings tight they will not fly away.

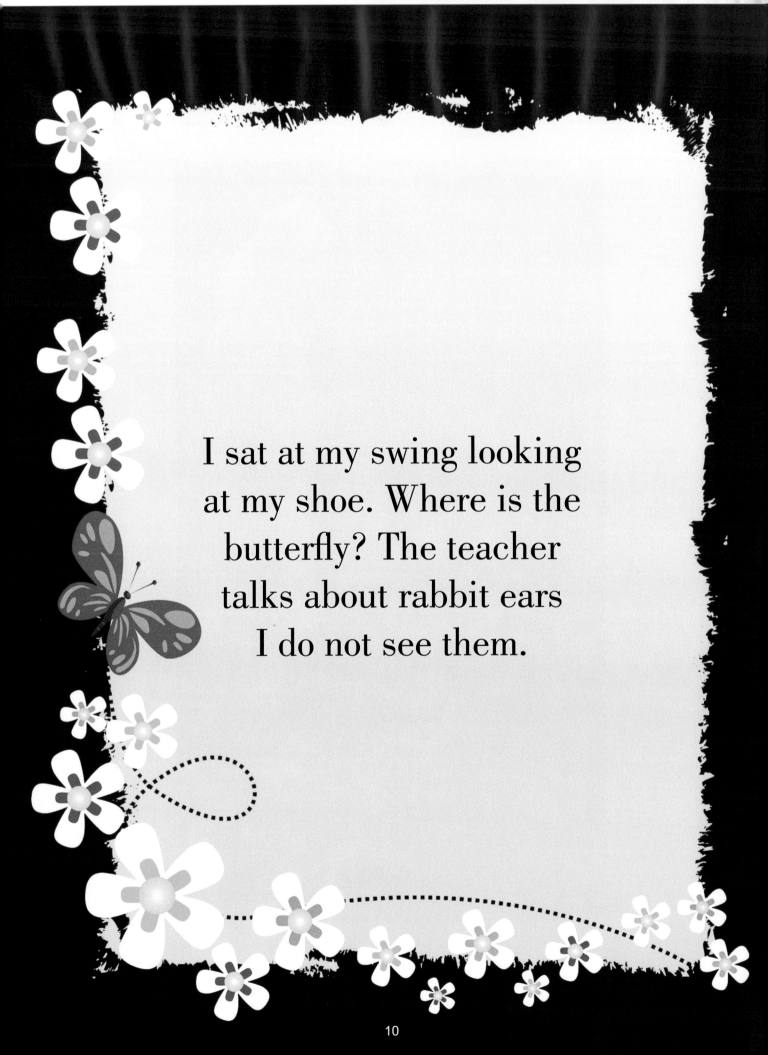

I sat at my swing looking at my shoe. Where is the butterfly? The teacher talks about rabbit ears I do not see them.

My older sister came to me
ask what wrong.

Can you help me?
Tie my shoe.

She sat behind me we
made an x with the laces.
Then we put one string
in the hole. I grab
both ends and pull
them tight.

With one lace I made a loop
then wrap the other lace just
once around the loop.

I then took the string
I wrapped around and made
a loop and pulled it threw
were I wrapped
it around.

Then I pulled both loops.

I TIED MY SHOE!!!

Printed in the United States
By Bookmasters